Portraits of Courageous Women

by Ardis O. Higgins

For Stewart G. Graham
Congratulations and Best Wishes
Sincerely, Ardis O. Higgins

 halls of ivy press

ISBN 0-912256-12-5

PUBLISHED BY

HALLS OF IVY PRESS

13050 Raymer St., North Hollywood, CA 91650

PRINTED IN U.S.A.

"The quality of greatness shines out like a beacon in the night; a word, a gesture, or a flashing glance may give the clue; then actions follow thought."

—MALVINA HOFFMAN

"Enter to learn. Depart to serve."

—MARY McLEOD BETHUNE

"You're not really a person until you've fulfilled yourself as an artist. You can't live until you've said what you have to say."

—LEONTYNE PRICE

Preface

Dear Young Readers:

As you read this book you will become acquainted with several fascinating women who really lived the interesting experiences told here.

There is a brave war correspondent, a night sky watcher who discovered a comet, an Indian woman who created a new pottery and shared her success with her Pueblo, a courageous group of Frontier Nurses, and many others.

They left a vast heritage of words and symbols, of ideas and of skills and talents.

There are the words of Mary McCleod Bethune, the black educator, who placed above the entrance of her primitive school the words, "Enter to learn. Depart to serve."

There is the symbol of good sportsmanship as lived by Babe Didrickson whose fine combination of mind and muscle produced such outstanding athletic skill was matched by a spirit of integrity and determination to compete and to win.

The ideas and creative planning for international leadership is expressed by the women who were elected from Africa to the Presidency of that important world organization called the United Nations.

The good deeds which helped to free her countrymen from poverty and ignorance were those of Catherine II the Great of Russia.

There is Leontyne Price, the black opera star, who said,

"You're not really a person until you've fulfilled yourself as an artist. You can't live until you've said what you have to say."

This doesn't mean that you must be an artist, musician, or a writer in order to "fulfill yourself as an artist, or, say what you have to say." It does mean, however, that you sincerely use your skills and talents and those hidden forces within you to create or achieve the greatest things possible in the very best way you know, or can learn, how to do. It may be playing a musical instrument, writing a poem or a story, or building a dog house for your best friend. Your special talent may be designing a dress or a skirt, preparing food from your own original recipes, coaching a younger friend to play tennis, or painting in a style of your very own that has genuine meaning for you and for those who will be looking at it.

The sculptress Malvina Hoffman used her skill to create many works whose impact on mankind has been as strong as the metal and stone from which they were made. Think about what she said about greatness. "The quality of greatness shines out like a beacon in the night; a word, a gesture, or a flashing glance may give the clue; then actions follow thought; Something new . . . unfolding beauty . . the soul unsheathes itself and flowers into being, creating an adventure."

The most humble girl or boy may have the quality of greatness. Even the poorest may show the finest spirit and courage. What makes them so? Perhaps some of the chapters of this book will help.

Understanding something about the life of these women may explain the meaning of words like integrity and justice, courage and dedication, creativity and determination, talent and persistence, sportsmanship and values. Only did those words have real meaning in the lives of these women when they were put to work in each of their lives.

We hope you will want to think about yourself as you read, about how your life might become full and harmonious as an individual and as a helpful and valuable person in your community.

Table of Contents

PREFACE V

MARIA MITCHELL
Skywatcher and discoverer of a comet 1

THE LOST WOMAN OF SAN NICHOLAS ISLAND
For 18 years the only human on the Island . . . 6

FRONTIER NURSES
Traveling on horseback, they treated the sick
and delivered babies 10

NETA SNOOK AND A. E.
One of the first woman pilots and her famous pupil . 14

HELEN, TRUDY AND BABE
Athletes who set the pace 18

MARIA POVEKA
Indian creator of a new pottery in San Ildefonso Pueblo 22

MALVINA HOFFMAN
Sculptress: The races of man and their cultures,
her specialties 25

FUMIKO MIYAGI
Artist of Japan and meals for her millions 30

KIRSTEN FLAGSTAD AND LEONTYNE PRICE
Firsts for American Opera 33

MARY McCLEOD BETHUNE
Schools for her people in the South 42

JULIA, FANNY AND CATHERINE
Cooks, cookbooks and kitchens 46

CATHERINE II THE GREAT
Wise Empress of Russia 50

ELINORE, THE HOMESTEADER
 American pioneer in the West 54

MARGUERITE HIGGINS, WAR CORRESPONDENT
 More front page stories than any other reporter . . 57

DEBORAH AND LYDIA
 Judge and Businesswoman of the Bible 60

UNITED NATIONS LEADERS
 At top of the world's organization 65

SOME NATIONAL CHARACTERISTICS . . . 68

THE FASHION WORLD OF AFRICA 69

THE BEDOUIN MAIDEN 72

THE JAPANESE BRIDE 75

Maria Mitchell, Astronomer
Skywatcher and discoverer of a comet

The night was cold, but the stars were bright in the clear dark sky above the rooftop. It was the hour for stargazing.

Maria climbed the ladder, following her father up to the roof where a telescope was set up each evening to observe the skies and the weather. Stargazing was very important in the little community on Nantucket Island, fifty miles off Boston, in 1831. Most of the houses had a "walk" on the roof, a small platform with a picket fence where families could watch ships coming and going in the harbor and look at the stars.

Maria's ancestors were members of the Society of Friends, known as Quakers, who had migrated from England to America. Maria was born in England on August 1, 1818.

Nantucket Island was a great whaling center, and the sailors steered their boats by the stars. Most of the men were away for days at a time, sometimes weeks and months because fishing was their main industry. Before the days of modern navigational instruments, sailors and fishermen observed the skies to learn of their location at sea and to predict the weather.

Maria's father was not a sailor. William Mitchell worked as a farmer, a teacher, and a banker. He became master of the first free school on Nantucket and later was appointed cashier, or principal officer of the Pacific Bank there. But he enjoyed most being an amateur astronomer. Sea captains frequently consulted him about the weather, and after each whaling voyage they brought him their chronometers for adjustment. Maria began helping her father rate those chronometers while still in her teens. This was done by checking them against her observations of the stars.

The ten Mitchell children had their early education in their own home and all helped out with the daily chores of the Quaker household. This included cleaning the whale-oil lamps which they carried up to the roof each evening with their chronometers and record books.

During an eclipse of the sun, when the moon passes in front of the sun and briefly turns day into night, they mounted the telescope in the parlor window. While her father observed through the long instrument, Maria, then twelve, counted the seconds by a clock so that the exact time of the eclipse could be recorded. This also aided in determining the exact longitude of Nantucket Island for maps of the United States. Maria spoke of this experience as giving her the feeling of being a part of an orderly universe.

When Maria was sixteen, she became an assistant teacher in the little Quaker school. At eighteen, she became librarian

of Nantucket's library called the Atheneum. Here many famous
people came to present lectures on scientific interests.

Maria continued to devote her evenings to stargazing and
helped her father build a shed on the roof to shelter their astronomical equipment. They were now using a four-inch telescope owned by the director of the Coast Survey. It had been
loaned to them so that they could send in observations from
their island which was one of the stations along the coast. Other
instruments were loaned to them by West Point Academy, and
the director of the Harvard Observatory went out to show them
how to use the equipment.

For the next ten years, Maria enjoyed recording their observations at night, helping with the housework in the morning and working at the library in the afternoons.

Suddenly, something happened on the evening of October
1, 1847, when Maria was alone on the roof. This was to change
the course of her life. Because her father had guests that evening, Maria dressed warmly and went up to make the evening's
observations alone. As she looked through the telescope, she saw
something completely new. It was a faint light just above the
star Polaris. That area had always been dark without any ob-
jects. What she was seeing was a white spot, and it was moving,
although very slowly. Maria was observing the first spectacle
of an unknown comet!

She rushed down to tell her father who immediately went
up to the roof and looked into the telescope. Then he recorded
the event in the official notebook. The chronometer showed
that the time was exactly ten-thirty.

Comets are not common spectacles, not even today. The
King of Denmark had offered to present a gold medal to any-
one who first sighted an unknown comet through a telecope.
It took a long time for the news to reach Europe because com-

munications across the ocean were very slow in 1847. But scientists around the world eventually became aware that a young lady on a tiny island off the coast of North America had discovered a comet before any of the great well known astronomers had seen it.

When the gold medal from the King of Denmark arrived, Maria became the first woman to receive the award. A Latin inscription was on it. When translated it meant, "Not in vain do we watch the setting and the rising of the stars."

A comet is always named for the person who discovers it, so the white spot sighted moving through the sky that October night became known as Maria Mitchell's Comet.

Maria became famous, and in 1848 was elected to membership in the American Academy of Arts and Sciences. Maria was the first woman to be admitted. In 1850, she became a member of the Association for the Advancement of Science, again she was the first woman. The director of the Smithsonian Institute sent her one hundred dollars with which she bought books. A group called Women of America gave her a new telescope. The following year, she began writing for the U.S. Nautical Almanac, a booklet which predicts movements of stars to help sailors on the open seas. Her special assignment was on the planet Venus.

After a trip to Europe, where she met many great people, she had an offer to become professor of astronomy at Vassar College, a new institute of learning for women only, which was opened in 1865. Her professorship there continued for twenty-three years. She retired just before her seventieth birthday, and died a year later on June 28, 1889 at Lynn, Massachusetts.

She was a teacher with imagination and methods in advance of her time and became one of Vassar's greatest teachers. When any special astronomical event occured, she would awaken the students in the middle of the night to see the phenomenon from the roof of the dormitory. Particularly memorable was a cold night in 1869 when falling meteors were counted by the hundreds and hot refreshments followed later in front of a glowing wood fire. Later Maria's "dome parties" became popular with little tables set around the big twelve-inch telescope in the new observatory.

In 1887, Columbia University conferred an honorary doctorate degree on Maria and her name was carved among the great names on the front of the Boston public library. An observatory on Nantucket was dedicated to her memory in 1910, and visitors from all over the world view the Maria Mitchell Museum at her former home on Nantucket.

In 1975 American astronauts landing on the moon would be using a map on which there was a crater named "Miss Mitchell's Comet".

The Lost Woman of San Nicholas Island
For 18 years the only human being on the Island

This is a true story of an Indian woman who lived alone on a deserted island for eighteen years and kept alive by catching fish, sea urchins, abalones, and lobsters. It is one of the most astounding true stories of one person's fight for survival ever recorded in the annals of time.

San Nicholas is a barran flat topped sandy island of about twenty square miles located off the coast of Southern California, seventy-six miles out to sea from Los Angeles Harbor. It is a bird island, populated by thousands of ravens, carmorants, sea gulls, blue herons, bald eagles, canaries, larks and robins. It is also the home of thousands of sea lions. The Island was named for the saint's day celebrated December 6, 1602, when the

Spainish explorer, Cabrillo, sailed by the island.

In the early 19th century, the Indians on the Island were plundered by otter hunters to such a degree that in 1835 the Franciscan padres who had set up Missions throughout California, decided to move the last of the Indians to the mainland. The schooner, Peores Nada, was chartered to bring them to San Pedro.

The captain of the small vessel was Charles Hubbard who conveyed the idea to the Indians that they would no longer be subjected to the cruelty of the otter hunters and that they would have plenty to eat and life would be better on the mainland.

As the Indians were piling their scant belongings into the vessel, a sudden gale threatened to hurl the boat against the rocky shores. One of the Indian women discovered that her child had not been brought aboard. She leaped into the water and swam ashore. Captain Hubbard, fearing for the safety of the vessel and the lives of those aboard, set sail across the choppy channel leaving the Indian Woman and the child alone on the isolated island. At Los Angeles Harbor, the Indians were met by Franciscans who assimilated them with other Indians at San Gabriel Mission.

Captain Hubbard planned to return to San Nicholas Island to get the Indian woman, but less than a month later he and the boat sank in San Francisco Bay. No one returned for the abandoned woman for fifteen years, thinking she could not possibly survive. Particularly dangerous were the vicious wild dogs, descendants of the animals loved by the Indian woman's forefathers.

In 1850, George Nidever and Thomas Jeffries with a crew of Indians, sailed to the small island to hunt otter, but also to look for the lost Indian woman. After six weeks, one of the Indians hurried into camp, telling of seeing a figure running in the distance. He tried, but could not catch her.

Three years later, George Nidever and Carl Detman were on another otter hunting excursion and this time they found a basket which contained a robe made of bird's feathers. They abandoned the otter hunting and concentrated on finding the woman. A few days later Detman discovered footprints and following them, was led to a grass shelter on one of the Island's peaks. She was seated inside, from were she could observe the hunters on the beach below. At her side was a pack of dogs, trained to respond to her commands immediately, and two pet ravens. She was dressed in cormorant feathers and she was in excellent physical condition with a large supply of food in her grass hut.

Through sign language she communicated with the men, explaining how her child had died, and how she had existed alone those eighteen years, hiding from all visitors. There was plenty of food and water from many little streams.

Thinking to befriend the woman, Nidever took her along when he returned to the mainland. His wife cared for the shy, quite, and attractive person. The Mission Fathers tried but were unsuccessful in locating one of her tribesmen who could speak the woman's language. In spite of the comforts of civilization, the Indian woman lived only three months after being removed from her Island. It has been assumed that the great contrast in diet may have caused her death.

As the last hours drew near, she was baptised by the Mission Padres who named her Juana Maria. Her robe was sent to the Pope in Rome where it can be seen in the Vatican Museum. In the Santa Barbara Mission graveyard, where she was buried, a placque was erected in 1928 which reads:

Juana Maria
· Indian Woman Abandoned on
San Nicholas Island eighteen years
Found and brought to
Santa Barbara
by
Captain George Nidver
in 1853
Santa Barbara Chapter
Daughters of the
American Revolution
1928

Those Frontier Nurses
Traveling on horseback, they treated the sick and
delivered babies

The narrow path up the mountain was so rough that the
horse stepped carefully and slowly. His rider, dressed in a blue-
gray uniform, held on tightly, her little medical kit hanging
from the saddle.

The horse and rider were on their way to an isolated region
in Kentucky to provide medical help. The rider belonged to the
Frontier Nursing Service and was on her way to assist in the
delivery of a new baby.

Because there were no roads, no electricity, nor even any
water piped into the log cabin homes, life in the rugged but
beautiful hills of the Appalachian mountains was very primitive.
Whenever illness occured or new babies were born, the isolated

families had no help except from the Frontier Nurses. And, of course, they had to come on horseback.

The nurse in the blue-gray uniform riding up Thousand-sticks Mountain was just as excited about the expected baby as was its family. The Frontier Nurses were devoted to the "Tuckies," their favorite name for the families who lived in the rural region of Kentucky.

There had not always been such medical help for the people in the mountains. Very primitive conditions existed before 1925 when Mrs. Mary Breckenridge took up the challenge against disease and the death of infants in that region. Inspired by the Frontier Nursing Service in Great Britain where she had done intensive study of nursing training in Britain and the Scottish highlands, she set out to create a similar program for the mountain people of Kentucky. She worked hard, bringing from Great Britain nurses experienced in giving medical aid to mountain people and in delivering babies.

Besides treating the sick and delivering babies, these nurses could superintend primitive carpenter work and well-digging. They took care of their own horses, advised about farming, and taught young girls to cook.

Their own living conditions were just as primitive. With no gas or electricity, they lived cheerfully by candlelight and bathed in a basin of water poured from a pitcher. If the washing water was to be warm, it had to be heated in buckets over a wood fire.

The mountain area was divided into geographic areas. Among the sixteen young nurses on duty, each one thought her own patients were the very best.

By 1928 a small hospital was built on the mountain overlooking Hyden, Kentucky. This and a large log cabin at nearby Wendover served as a center for the Frontier Nursing Service.

But primitive conditions existed at the hospital too. Even a refrigerator was run, not by electricity or gas, but by a motor operated by kerosene.

Something very special happened each morning. Music was heard over the mountainside when a hymn was played on a trumpet by the resident nurse-midwife at Wendover.

One day a visitor who walked miles over mountain paths came to see Wendover and the hospital near Hyden. During lunch, which was served at a table near a large window, fascinating stories were told of the exciting work.

Suddenly, one of the nurses pointed toward the big window and shouted, "It's a boy!"

Down the mountain someone was approaching on horseback. As she came closer, her blue-gray uniform could be identified. Everyone was happy, waiting for the details. For the news of each new birth amid the "Tuckies" was a joyous event for all.

But how did they know it was a boy? She was carrying no lettered sign, nor was she within calling distance. Besides her medical bag, the only unusual thing on the saddle was a huge branch of the most beautifully colored fall leaves.

And then came the explanation of the rules for announcements of the new born — bunches of wide flowers if it's a girl, branches of colored leaves if it's a boy.

At that time, the only nurse-midwives (those nurses allowed to deliver babies) in the United States were trained in Great Britain. But during World War II, in the late 1930's, many of the British nurses asked to go home to serve their own country which was involved in the war. Without any trained nurses left, Mary Breckenridge set up the Frontier Nursing School of Midwifery under the Health Department of the state of Kentucky which licensed the nurses. The course was planned after the six month course for graduate nurses given in Great Britain.

From those first sixteen nurses from Great Britain grew the American Association of Nurse-midwives. Originating in Kentucky in 1928, it grew to over 250 who are scattered all over the world. Once a year they return to the rugged and beautiful mountainous region where they served the "Tuckies."

Now there are roads cut through the mountain brush, and horses have been exchanged for jeeps. Many people prefer to come to the little hospital on the mountainside for treatment. A chapel, started by one dollar from many of the 12,000 babies who had been delivered by the Frontier Nursing Service, was built next to the hospital.

Visitors from all over the world come to study the Service started by that single courageous woman. They come to get advice on how to plan their own rural nursing service.

A new hospital was built on level ground in 1967 in memory of Mrs. Mary Breckenridge, whose idea, desire, and strong determination will live on in the Frontier Nursing Service.

Neta Snook and A. E.
One of the first women pilots and her famous pupil

In those days no one ever heard of jet planes or 747's because flying was a new venture. But there she was, tinkering with the engine of a small airplane. Her cropped hair made a frame for her grease smeared face, and, in one hand she was holding a wrench.

Neta Snook had been working for many hours on her plane. She was anxious to keep the engine working properly because she had several flying students scheduled that week, and there were not many good airplane mechanics in those days.

She had a reputation as an outstanding flier and an excellent teacher. Neta Snook was known as a woman who flied as well as any man, in spite of her petite size.

When a slim young woman appeared for her first lesson

one day, she was told to hop in. Eagerly the young student called out, "I'm ready."

Grinning at her, Neta Snook said, "Oh, we're not going to fly right away. You have a lot to learn right here on the ground before you can go up."

That was one of the reasons Neta Snook was such a good instructor. She prepared her students thoroughly on the ground before they ever had to tackle unknown situations in the air. First they had to learn the various parts of the plane and what each one did. When her young students were ready to fly, Neta Snook would sit in back of them and let them pilot the plane because it had dual controls.

Neta Snook was probably the first woman pilot in the United States when she learned to fly in 1917. But in those days before she could learn to fly, she had to learn to build the plane.

One time a young woman student whom we will call by the initials A. E. was at the controls in the air. While trying to land she dumped them in a cabbage patch. Coming down closer and closer to the ground they landed with such a bump that the propeller and the landing gear were damaged. A. E. was terribly embarrassed and very worried.

Neta Snook merely complimented her on having the good sense to cut the switch and turn off the engine. A. E. asked her why she had not taken over the controls in the air when she saw that they were going to crash. Calmly, Neta Snook explained that there really had been no great danger. She had wanted her student to learn to handle everything herself, even in case of a crash.

A. E. was to remember that lesson the rest of her life for she became one of the greatest women pilots who made flying records and flew alone over both the Atlantic and Pacific Oceans. A. E., of course, stands for Amelia Earhart.

Amelia Earhart was to earn as fine a reputation for flying as her teacher, Neta Snook. She was to gain even more popularity and admiration for her courageous and daring exploits in behalf of aviation.

One dark stormy night in the spring of 1932 Amelia was flying all alone over the Atlantic Ocean, her plane tossing and shaking in the rough wind. Glancing at the altimeter gauge which would tell her how high above the stormy waves she was flying she saw the hands in the dial swinging back and forth. The altimeter was broken! Now she could not tell how high or how low she was flying.

The night grew darker and the storm blew harder. Thunder and lightning crashed across the sky in jagged streaks. She was having a hard time keeping the plane under control. So she tried to climb above the storm where it might be more calm. But ice formed on the wings making the plane so heavy that it went into a spin, dropping in a straight line right toward the ocean three thousand feet below. Amelia managed to level off just before hitting the waves. In the lower and warmer air near the ocean the ice began to melt and she could lift the plane again.

Amelia had been flying for about ten hours from her take-off on the American continent. She was not quite sure just where she was, but she did know there were at least another three anxious hours before she could reach the shores of Great Britain, her goal.

The first person to fly alone across the Atlantic Ocean was Charles Lindbergh, at the age of 25. He astonished the whole world with his miraculous flight from New York to Paris in 1927.

Now Amelia hoped her plane would be able to handle the rough stormy weather. In the five years since Lindbergh's flight, aviation had provided pilots with instruments which he did not have on his long solo of 33½ hours.

In spite of instruments, problems were mounting for Amelia. Her altimeter was broken, a flame had flickered several times from the engine, and one of her gas tanks was leaking.

Finally came the morning light of dawn. The heavy clouds below her plane were so bright that she had to put on dark glasses, but she could not see through the masses of clouds. So she flew lower to get in the shade under the clouds, and there on the water below she spotted a ship. What a feeling of relief! That might indicate she was near land, if she stayed on course.

When the coastline of Ireland finally became visible she scanned the countryside for a railroad line to follow, or an airfield. None were in sight. But her faithful though battered plane had to be landed as soon as possible. Then she saw a fairly level green pasture. Flying lower she saw grazing cattle, and after circling several times to find the best place to land, she finally set the plane down.

It was a safe landing, and her goal was accomplished. She had become the first woman in the world to fly across the Atlantic Ocean alone.

Amelia Earhart was involved in man achievements in behalf of aviation. She was also the first woman to fly solo from Hawaii to the United States. Then in 1937 she started out on an around-the-world flight from west to east. It was on one of the last portions of the trip while flying from New Guinea near Australia to the United States that she was lost and vanished in the Pacific Ocean.

Helen, Trudy and Babe

Athletes who set the pace

They were Helen, Trudy and Babe, those first American women to become internationally famous in the field of sports!

It is a fairly new thing, this recognition of women as athletes. Only since 1900 have women been encouraged to participate to any great extent in the international events called the Olympics.

On the tennis courts in the early 1900's, women in long, heavily starched cotton skirts with black belts, long-sleeved shirts, and a man's black tie and stockings, played a game in perfect conformity with the rules of propriety and etiquette.

Helen Wills, remembered as America's greatest tennis queen, changed all that. She learned to play tennis as a little girl because her best friend, a boy, liked the game better than anything else. And encouraged by her father, a sports-loving doctor, she became the only American Woman to win an Olympic gold medal for single play in tennis. She also won the two most important titles in women's tennis, the U.S. Nationals and Wimbledon, played in England.

However, Helen Wills, a talented and versatile person, a brilliant student, an art major, and the recipient of the Phi Betta Kappa key for excellence in college, was a devotee of healthy living, sensible practice hours, and good tennis strategy. She was to become the liberator for women of the impediment of long skirts, long sleeves, and long stockings. In 1927 she appeared in short skirts, sleeveless shirts, and no stockings, at all, and created a sensation. The irate public wanted her rebuked for her uncovered calves. The following year, the first shorts appeared for women.

Gertrude "Trudy" Ederle of New York City, was 19 years old in 1926 when she became the first woman in history to swim the twenty miles across the English Channel in the record-breaking time of 14 hours, 31 minutes. Only five men had conquered the Channel. The previous record, held by an Argentinian was 16½ hours.

Because the water of the Channel was bitterly cold, even in summer, six pounds of thick, black grease were smeared over her body to protect her from the cold. Warm beverages were slipped over the side of the accompanying French tug named Alsace, and three of the world's finest swimmers occasionally dove in to encourage her with their strong, fresh strokes. Tides, winds, and battering salt spray added to make the challenge even greater. Her trainer knew the rigors of the swim, for he had tried 19 times before becoming the second person to beat the Channel.

It had been 7:08 a.m., French summer time, when she waded into the sea at Cape Griz-Nez, France, to begin the trek. As she approached the coast of England, darkness was setting in and brilliant flares of red, green, and blue lit the horizon. At exactly 9:39 p.m. Gertrude Ederle waded out of the water at Kingsdown, England onto the crowded beach, becoming the first woman to swim the English Channel, and to beat the men's record.

In searching for the Woman Athlete of the Half-Century in 1950, almost unanimously among the nation's sports writers, the choice was Babe Didrikson. She was considered the most talented athlete, male or female, and the most versatile, playing at several different sports. She had been a basketball star, Olympic gold medalist in track and field, and a national and international champion in amateur and professional golf. She also excelled in every other sport she tried. And she could sew, cook, type and dance as well as most women.

Born of Norwegian immigrant parents in Port Arthur, Texas, in 1914, Mildred Didrikson grew up in a close-knit, loving family of seven children, and learned to enjoy the vitality of an active sports life with her brothers.

Native athletic ability alone does not lead to championships without persistence, endurance and devotion to practice. The Babe spent hours and months in training as she prepared for her numerous competitions. One of these was the Los Angeles Open Golf in 1938 where she was teamed up with a Presbyterian Minister and George Zaharias, a noted wrestler, who was to become her husband within a year.

In two seasons, 1946 and 1947, she set an all time record by winning nineteen straight golf championships.

At the height of her career in 1953 she discovered she had cancer. One year after major surgery, with courage and per-

severance, she regained her championship form winning the
All-American Golf Tournament.

In 1956 when America's greatest woman athlete died, she
had won the respect and admiration of the entire sports world
for her physical and spiritual courage.

Maria the Potter
Indian creator of a new pottery in San Ildefonso Pueblo

On the bottom of one little black bowl the name "MA-RIE" was visible. Another was signed "MARIE AND JUL-IAN". A third one had the signature, "MARIE POVEKA". But who was Marie?

Maria, the potter who made black-on-black bowls famous, is probably one of the first American Indian women to gain recognition, not only in America, but throughout the world. She lived in the Indian Pueblo Villiage, San Ildefonso, in New Mexico.

Maria had great charm, beauty, and simple graciousness, a strong character and keen intellect. She was born Maria Montoya about 1881. She also used her Indian name for autographs, Maria Poveka. In 1904 she married Julian Martinez who was to share in the excitement of creating an artistic product for which their whole Indian tribe would become famous.

Maria's earliest pottery was made for use in the pueblo as water jars, seed bowls, storage ollas, meat bowls, double-necked wedding jars, and other utility bowls. The first actual sales of Maria's work brought three dollars for a large bowl and a dollar and a half for a small bowl. White men, friends who had hired Julian to work for them in building the first museum in Santa Fe, were her first customers. They introduced her ware to the early tourists and visitors to New Mexico. Later, between the years 1908 and 1912 when Julian was hired as maintenance man of the museum, Maria was invited to demonstrate her ware there in Santa Fe.

Since pottery making is commonly done by the women of a pueblo, some of her relatives also sought a commercial outlet for their pots. It was this opportunity which Maria provided that opened a whole new economy for the entire pueblo.

The earliest pottery was black and red on cream. The unique black-on-black ware for which Maria and Julian became famous was the result of accident and experimentation with the outdoor firing of the pots about 1919. For two years they kept their secret method of producing the black ware, but in 1921, at the request of relatives and friends, they taught others in the San Ildefonso Pueblo how to make the unique color.

In those earliest days, no signatures appeared on the ware, but as the white merchants realized the slight differences, they urged Maria to sign her pieces, which she did about 1923. It was their suggestion to use the name Marie, rather than Maria. Some were signed Marie, but about 1925 the signatures Marie and Julian appeared, since Maria wanted him to receive recognition for decorating the pots. However, some unsigned pieces appeared as late as 1926.

Her work attracted attention of the whole world as early as the St. Louis Fair when she and her husband, Julian, were set up in a replica of their vlliage home to show the attractive black ware. With the same fine sand and clay brought from the hills of New Mexico they demonstrated their method of reviving the ancient Pueblo craft of pottery making.

Today those little black pieces, whatever the signature, are valuable almost beyond measure, for they reveal a definite period in the craftsmanship of the artistic ability of the American Indians.

If you were to visit the San Ildefonso Pueblo you would find there the exclusive outlet for Maria's work in the Studio of Indian Arts run by members of her family.

Among American Indian artists, Maria was the first woman to be honored by the Indian Council Fire with the Indian Achievement Award in 1934. Her artistry and research in producing black pottery and the instruction of others in her pueblo is well known. She received the craftsman medal from the American Institute of Architects in 1954 and the Jane Addams medal for Distinguished Service to Mankind from Rickford College in 1959. Honorary degrees were conferred by the Universities of Colorado and New Mexico. At the age of ninety in April of 1975, during a visit with this author, Maria delighted in recalling her four visits to the White House with Presidents Hoover, Roosevelt, Eisenhower and Johnson.

Malvina Hoffman

Sculptress: The races of man and their cultures, her specialties.

Using a pencil, a wooden spool, a shoe-horn and some hairpins the young girl made an armature for her sculpture.

As a child, Malvina Hoffman was interested in mechanical toys and enjoyed working with her hands. Her father, Richard Hoffman, who was a piano teacher and the piano soloist with the New York Philharmonic Orchestra for thirty years, encouraged her artistic and creative ability.

They spent many hours together talking about the life of an artist. On long walks they would study buildings and how they were made. Malvina would make little sketches putting in all the details of the buildings and the horses and carriages they passed.

Malvina was born in 1885 in New York City and died there in 1966. As a teenager, she attended art school in addition to her regular school. During subway and trolley rides to the art school, she would make quick sketches of the passengers.

For six years she worked with paints and brushes. Then one day, feeling very sad about a tragedy that happened to a friend, she modeled a small clay figure of a lonely woman bowed with grief. Beginning with a pencil stuck into a large wooden spool and a metal shoe-horn lashed to it with twisted hairpins, she made the armature or skeleton to hold the clay for the figure. Then she added soft lumps of the clay with her fingers to make the lonely figure.

After making several paintings of her father in color, Malvina wanted to do a three dimentional head in clay, so he agreed to pose for her. To reveal the true character of the face of a figure, Malvina discovered that it became necessary to make many profiles modeled in clay from every view around the head, from the front, back, sides, above and below. Only then would the form appear to be actually living.

Malvina's clay head of her father was giving her trouble. The shoulders would not hold their shape. When the famous Danish sculptor, Gutzon Borglum came to visit, he asked what had been put inside. Malvina told him she had used three sticks of kindling wood fastened to a base, a tin can upside down over the top, and a short board tied across to hold the shoulders. The great sculptor who had carved the four faces of the presidents at the Rushmore Monument on the mountainside in South Dakota, decided to teach her how to construct a proper armature. He used pieces of iron pipe screwed to a wooden base and short bits of wood wired together as cross pieces. When Malvina applied the clay the result was excellent.

This encouragement of Gutzon Borglum helped her decide to become a sculptress.

After viewing the figure, her father said, "My child, I'm afraid you're going to be an artist. It's a long, hard road and you have to travel most of the time entirely alone... Above all, you must BE an artist; after that you may create art."

Malvina was encouraged to have a plaster model made of the bust of her father so that she could carve it in marble. This was her first experience carving in stone. The finished piece was so good that it was accepted and exhibited at the National Academy of Design in New York.

After her father died in 1910, Malvina went to Europe for further study. In Paris she became a studio helper to an American sculptor, Janet Scudder, and studied the figures at the famous Louvre Museum. Her one desire was to work with the great French sculptor Auguste Rodin. Malvina made several attempts to see him. Rodin finally looked at her work and immediately took her on as a pupil guiding her through many months of extremely difficult and exacting work. Malvina learned everything she could about all the phases of sculpture including watching the work in the foundry where her figures were cast into bronze.

To create the perfect figure, a sculptor must understand thoroughly the anatomy of the body and experience the type of movement her figure is expressing. To learn about the human body, Malvina enrolled as a student in the College of Physicians and Surgeons in New York. To personally experience body movements, particularly in ballet, she took dancing lessons from the best teachers of the Russian ballet.

She was so fascinated with the ballet that she made a bronze group of the famous dancers Anna Pavlova and Mikhail Mordkin in a pose from the lively "Bacchanale" dance. Following the sculpture was a frieze of twenty-six panels which present the beauty and detailed action of the entire dance.

Several years later in Geneva, Switzerland, her skill in projecting personality was made evident when she created a set of four busts of Ignace Paderewski, the famous composer-pianist, whom she had heard play in New York when she was a child. Paderewski was then the Premire of Poland in 1920. She called the four pieces of sculpture "The Statesman," "The Man," "The Artist," "The Friend."

In 1923, Malvina was commisioned to create a symbol of American and English friendship to be placed over the Bush House, a nine-story office building in London. Under an arch at the very top of the building she assembled huge stone male figures holding between them a torch over an altar. Malvina was such a dedicated artist that when the additional carving had to be done on the faces after they were assembled high on the building, she did it herself. Climbing up the ninety feet above the street, she sat astride the shoulders of the big figure and worked on the lines of the face.

To sculpt is exciting. To produce sculpture which promotes universal brotherhood is challenging and rewarding. Malvina Hoffman produced that kind of sculpture.

She could create a delicate and graceful African dancing girl as well as a sturdy and daring Hawiian surf rider. To model from life all the races of mankind, she traveled throughout the world to study differences in human bodies, in their faces, and in their actions. When these bronze figures were completed they were placed in the Hall of Man at the Field Museum of Chicago which is now called the Chicago Natural History Museum.

One of her last projects combined two of her greatest interests, sculpture and medicine. To express the origin and history of medicine, she designed thirteen stone reliefs for the outside walls for Dr. Joslin's Boston Hospital for Diabetes

Malvina Hoffman's talents were not limited to art and sculpture. She was also an interesting writer. In her book, *Heads and Tales*, she described her trip around the world to create the Hall of Man figures. In *Sculpture Inside and Out*, she wrote about her art. In *Yesterday Is Tomorrow*, she told of her personal and artistic life.

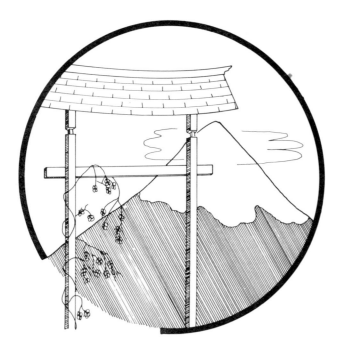

Fumiko Miyagi

Artist of Japan and meals for her millions

Her name is poetry itself, this woman who is many things to many people —

artist, humanitarian, adopted aunt, benefactor, educator, administrator, international hostess, writer, and recognized world citizen.

Art students at the university in Tokyo love her for her thoughtful attention to their endeavors. Collegues look forward to her innovations and stimulating suggestions. Friends, East and West, around the globe respect her intellectual curiosity and its applications. Guests in her homeland are overwhelmed at the numerous considerations and courtesies arranged in their behalf by this quiet woman whose motto might long ago have been heralded as "Others."

Fumiko-san is truly an artist—in color, design, and spirit. She sees the beautiful, creates an image, corrects the possible error, and attempts the genuinely perfect situation. Four small paintings on my wall express her love for color in nature. She has captured the lacy elegance of a spray of purple wisteria, the strong simplicity of a yellow lily, the lush pink excitement of cherry blossoms, and the delicate lavendar lilac blossoms of a tiny bonzai plant.

In her private and professional life, Fumiko Miyagi has always been concerned for the individual as well as for the masses. Dozens of middle-aged Japanese owe their very lives to Fumiko-san, who, during and immediately after World War II, opened the door of her Tokyo cottage and became both mother and father to bewildered orphaned chidren. Today, though scattered about the globe, she lives in their hearts as a favorite Adopted Aunt.

A major part of her energies in recent years have been driven to eradicate the hunger and malnutrition among young and old in her native Japan. Whenever her duties as professor of art in Tokyo permit, she travels to the rural areas of her native land investigating conditions and the delivery of the special foodstuffs from the international organization of which she is so proud.

As Founding President of Meals for Millions in that land of bullet trains, rice paddies, and cherry blossoms, Fumiko-san has been fighting famine by seeking funds, organizing communities, and investigating conditions of the soybean product produced as a dietary supplement to counteract the malnutrition of the thousands who are living under famine conditions in both rural and urban Japan.

An Honorary Doctorate of Human Letters from her alma mater in the United States contains these words:

FUMIKO MIYAGI, native of Japan, a graduate of the class of 1924, is truly an international figure. Her activity in art, her compassion for youth, her concern for the underfed have been channeled through teaching and association administration into effective humanitarian projects.

With admiration and appreciation . . . North Central College confers the degree of Doctor of Humane Letters, May 26, 1968.

Kirsten Flagstad and Leontyne Price
Firsts for American Opera

Say those names slowly and listen to the rhythmic poetry of their sound. Those musical names suggest the kind of gift these two women brought to the world.

Kirsten Flagstad

The excited lady stood at the rail of the big ship and peered through the fog. Somewhere in that gray mist was supposed to be the coastline of America.

Slowly the mist thinned out, and the fog began to lift. Then suddenly there it was! The New York skyline with its tall buildings, and standing nearby in the harbor welcoming her was the Statue of Liberty, symbol of American freedom.

Kirsten Flagstad's destination in America was the stage of

the Metropolitan Opera Company in New York City.

Speaking of her arrival after a week at sea of terrific fog she said, "As the fog lifted, it was like a scene from the Arabian Nights. Manhattan was all lighted up. The fog was like a curtain that had gone up on an opera scene."

Kirsten Flagstad had sung on several of the important opera stages in Europe, and now she was scheduled to sing at the "Met" as it was fondly known by opera lovers in America. This was one of the greatest achievements of any opera singer in the world.

In spite of the prestige the Metropolitan Opera had acquired it was in trouble at home financially. That day when Kirsten Flagstad of Norway arrived in America the people were beginning to recover from a great economic depression throughout the land. Few were able to buy tickets to attend operas when they did not have enough money for food and housing.

But Kirsten Flagstad had arrived from Norway. Extremely talented and musically inspiring, she reopened theater doors and filled the galleries.

Although she had established a fine reputation as a singer in Europe, no one was quite prepared for the fascinating quality of her voice and her great knowledge of opera. At her very first rehearsal the conductor who was directing the orchestra dropped his baton in amazement, and the lead male singer was so astonished that he missed his cue.

Madame Flagstad laughed as she spoke of that first reception on the American Stage, "They liked me . . . Back home I was just another singer."

Because the story of an opera is portrayed through its music an opera star must know not only her songs called "arias" and "recitatives," but she must know what the other characters on stage are supposed to do. There is often a large chorus of people on stage who also belong to the story. And then in front and below the stage is the orchestra and the conductor who directs the entire performance from the orchestra pit.

Madame Flagstad seldom needed to rehearse her roles. She knew them very well. She had been singing opera tunes since she was a young girl, and she had performed on many stages, especially in the Scandanavian countries and at the famous Bayreuth Opera House in Germany. Like the twist in an opera story she was preparing to retire from singing to a quiet life at home in Norway when Americans discovered her for the Metropolitan in New York. On February 2, 1935, her performance in the role of Sieglinde in the opera "Die Walkure" was one of the biggest box office attractions ever known in New York.

One of her most famous characters was named Brunnehilde, her heroine in several operas by Richard Wagner. Because of her brilliant performances she made the Wagner operas very popular in America. Opera lovers began crowding the opera houses, ticket sales increased, and once more, opera in the United States was overcoming its financial troubles. No one had generated that much enthusiam for opera, nor created the important and much needed box office returns, called money. Since then opera performances have continued to thrill audiences in America.

Kirsten Flagstad was born in Hamar, Norway, on July 12, 1895. Her father and mother, both professional musicians, had met while playing together in a small orchestra. They came from sturdy Norwegian peasant stock. From her earliest childhood, Kirsten was surrounded by music as both a household pleasure and a regular livelihood.

Growing up in a home where Norway's finest opera singers were being coached each day by her mother, young Kirsten was frequently called in to assist in a duet or some contrasting role during the coaching period. Her father was conductor of the opera in Oslo. But Kirsten had no thought of singing as a profession. Her interests were similar to those of other young women in Norway in the early 1900's. She wished to be happily married and to raise a family.

Very early in her life Kirsten became acquainted with the music of Richard Wagner when on her tenth birthday she was given a score of his opera "Lohengrin." Even at that age she learned the entire role of Else, all unaware that she would be singing and portraying Else on many stages in many countries later in her lifetime.

When she was eighteen Kirsten made her opera debut. She sang the role of a young girl named Nuri in the opera "Tiefland." At the first orchestra rehearsal the conductor tapped on the desk with his baton and said to the musicians, "Gentlemen, I think we should all feel honored. Miss Flagstad is the only one who has not made a single mistake in the whole rehearsal."

On the day of the performance she made herself an evening dress to wear to a debut party in a restaurant after the performance. Feeling very grown-up and with everyone congratulating her she considered it one of the biggest days of her whole life. When her first check arrived she bought new window curtains for her living room at home.

Young Kirsten loved sports as much as she did music. Her favorites were skiing and swimming. Living in Norway where the long winters provide plenty of snow on the mountains and in the valleys, Kirsten could be seen descending a hill in a swish of flying snow as dramatic a feminine figure as the roles she played on the opera stages

Critics were to refer to Kirsten Flagstad as . . . master of her art . . . the voice of the century . . . the world's most dramatic soprano.

In 1953 she retired in Norway to give charity concerts, and in 1958 she became the first director of the newly founded Norwegian Opera in Oslo.

Then, for the second time, when music in America was suffering from financial pressures, Kirsten Flagstad came again to these shores. Out of retirement she came from Norway to the aide of the famous NBC Orchestra which she had loved so much and with whom she had sung under the famous conductor Toscanini. He had retired, and the orchestra was then badly in need of money if it was to continue existing.

She paid her own way back to the United States to perform. Six hours after the morning papers announced her coming, tickets were completely sold out for that gala Sunday night, March 20, 1955. It was a glorious occasion. The audience and critics were thrilled and considered her still one of the world's greatest opera stars.

A recording of that performance was made which has become a valued collector's treasure.

LEONTYNE PRICE

At the time that Kirsten Flagstad was making her debut with the Metropolitan Opera Company in New York in 1935 there was a little girl in Laurel, Mississippi, who was singing and playing the piano for her family and friends and showing unusual musical talent.

Her name was Leontyne Price, and some years later she would sing on that same opera stage in New York City. But when she did she would be making history, not only musically, but socially! She was to break three important records at the Metropolitan.

First, Leontyne Price became the first black singer to star on the Metropolitan Opera Stage, but not until 1961. Second, she received the longest ovation of admiration from the audience that anyone ever had. Third, she was selected to sing the leading role on the opening night of the new and glamorous Opera House in 1965.

Leontyne came from a modest, black family in Mississippi. They lived on the money earned by her father who worked at a sawmill and by her mother who was a midwife helping to deliver babies. But when Leontyne displayed a talent for music, even at the age of four-and-a-half, she was given piano lessons and practiced on a toy piano. When her parents could not afford the two dollars for the lesson, Mrs. Price would do the teacher's washing and ironing.

Although Leontyne's father was not as enthusiastic as her mother regarding music lessons he did agree to trade their old record player as down payment on a real piano. But he was finally convinced when the little girl gave a piano recital at the age of five and had memorized every piece.

She also liked to sing and sang for many weddings and funerals in her home town.

Leontyne decided to become a music teacher. After high school she went to college up north, assisted financially by a member of a distinguished white family in her home town for whom she had sung many times, Mrs. Alexander Chisholm. Eventually Leontyne earned a Bachelor of Science degree at Central State College in Wilberforce, Ohio, graduating "cum laude," with honors. She won a scolarship for further music study at the famous Julliard School of Music in New York. While there she lived at the International House across the street and worked at the information desk.

The first opera Leontyne ever saw was "Turandot" at the City Center in New York. At the next one, "Salome," in the

Metropolitan Opera House, she had to stand the entire time because all the seats were sold out.

Leontyne was so entranced by what she saw and heard that she decided then to give up her plans to become a teacher for a career as an opera singer.

When she appeared in student performances music critics and composers realized her capabilities. Many invitations came to sing the leading roles in several important operas. Among them was "Porgy and Bess" composed by George Gershwin. She sang the part of Bess for two years in New York and then in Europe on a United States State Department cultural exchange tour. While on tour she studied for a career in opera, learning all the soprano roles fitted to her voice.

The beginning of her rise to stardom began quite by accident. During a performance of "Aida" in which she was not scheduled, the leading soprano became ill and had an emergency operation. Leontyne substituted in the emergency, and sang the leading role of "Aida" for which her voice was a perfect match. In 1951 a renowned European conductor, Herbert von Karojan, invited her to the great city of Vienna, Austria, to star in "Aida." This led to many more appearances in Europe.

Leontyne made her grand opera debut at the San Francisco Opera House in an opera by Poulene called "Dialogue of the Carmelites." In 1955 she became the first black to appear in opera on television in the opera "Tosca."

The dream of every great opera singer is to be invited to the famous Metropolitan Opera House in New York. For Leontyne her dream was to come true on January 27, 1961, when she appeared in the leading role of Leonora in Verdi's opera "Il Trovatore."

When she finished singing the audience gave her the longest ovation ever witnessed at the Metropolitan. For a full forty-two minutes they applauded with admiration.

A new Metropolitan Opera House was built in 1965 with dazzling fountains, elegant arches, gilded rafters, and crystal chandeliers. Brilliantly painted murals and fascades set off an audience dressed as though they were attending a royal coronation.

The opening event for such a building is always important. The stars selected to perform on its stage must be the greatest in the world, and the opera to be produced must be special for the occasion.

For this opening night and crowning event one of America's greatest composers, Samuel Barber, was commissioned to write an opera, and the soprano he chose to star in it was Leontyne Price. It was titled "Anthony and Cleopatra." This has been called the greatest musical honor to be accorded anyone in centuries, and Leontyne Price, a black woman from a modest Mississippi family, was the chosen one.

When she was asked to sing the leading role for that spectacular opening she was indeed the "Prima Donna Assoluta" of the international musical world, as the music critics had acclaimed. This means the first lady of opera.

As the giant curtains parted she stepped on to the stage and into history. It was the climax of her career. It was a personal triumph earned through years of hard work and much self-discipline. A glorious moment for all black people!

Her name has been hidden in crossword puzzles, and she has been the Cover Girl on numerous magazines. She has been voted Musician-of-the-Year and called the Girl of the Golden Voice. She has won many Grammy Awards and been named Best Classical Vocal Soloist several times for her recordings.

Leontyne Price is the only opera star to have received

America's highest civil award presented by President Johnson in 1964. He said, "Her singing has brought light to the world." In 1965 she was the only American to be decorated with the Italian award of Merit for her contribution to Italian music.

She is still a popular woman in her home town. When visiting in Laurel she goes to see her former teachers and sings at services at the churches. She inspires the young people to go to school and encourages others to study music.

The great star's new ambition is to "Add more dimensions to my life, to give of my time and myself to others, especially the youth." She discovered early in her career what she so eloquently has expressed to others, "You're not really a person until you've fulfilled yourself as an artist. You can't live until you've said what you have to say."

The great respect with which she is held by heads of government and with which she in turn holds them was evident at the close of a song recital one evening in Santa Barbara, California. After an evening of art songs, opera, and negro spirituals she graciously bade farewell, expressing regret at not being able to remain after the concert to greet friends. Outside, a black limosine was waiting to rush her to the Los Angeles airport for a night flight to Washington, D.C., where she was to sing the next morning at the funeral of a dear friend, President Lyndon B. Johnson.

Mary McLeod Bethune, Pioneer Teacher

Schools for the people in the south

"Put that book down. You can't read," the little white playmate said to Mary McLeod, the black child whose mother was doing the washing for the white girl's family.

The rebuke made about the book only served to stimulate the little black girl's natural intellectual curiosity. During the walk home with her mother Mary decided that although no one in her family could read, she would somehow, someday learn.

That evening, sitting at the knee of her grandmother, she asked questions of the wise old woman who had known for some time that this little black girl would someday accomplish great things for her people. One day she would take her first train ride, make sweet potato pies to sell and build a college which would bear her own name, Mary McLeod Bethune.

Born in a log cabin in South Carolina, Mary Jane was usually the last to wash each morning in the big wooden tub on the back porch since she was one of the youngest of the seventeen McLeod children. After breakfast they all went out to work on their father's farm where time was measured by the planting, weeding, and picking of cotton.

Patsy and Samuel, Mary's mother and father, had been slaves before the Civil War, but President Abraham Lincoln had set them free by the Emancipation Proclamation. Patsy had worked on the Wilson plantation, and Samuel belonged to the McLeods. When they were married, after Samuel had earned extra money to buy Patsy for himself, they took their master's name, McLeod, for their own. Slaves in those days had only first names. Thus little black Mary Jane McLeod, whose mother was a descendant of an African prince, carried the name of a white plantation owner whose descendants came from Scotland.

Schools for blacks in the south were almost unknown. In 1886, when Mary was eleven years old, the first school for black children in that part of South Carolina, was established three miles from Mary's log cabin home. But the little one room school was open only four months of the year. Mary became one of the best students and learned to read the Bible to her family. It was the only book they owned and it had been a gift from their preacher.

Because of her alert mind and determination, Mary was selected to receive education and was sent to a boarding school many miles away. Later she came back to that small village and became the teacher in the local school house, then open only two months a year.

Realizing that teaching was meant to be her life work, she applied for a full time position through the Presbyterian Board of Missions and was assigned to the Haines Institute in Atlanta, Georgia.

Some years later, while teaching at Kendall Institute at Sumpter, Mary met another teacher, Alburtus Bethune, who was to become her husband and the father of her son, Albert.

Mary began to think that she wanted a school of her own. Black families were moving to Daytona, Florida to work in the railroad yards. Mary decided that was a place where children would be needing a school. She went out and found an old unoccupied house near the ocean. Since sweet potatoes grew abundantly and were cheap, Mary made sweet potato pies and sold them at the work camps and in front of the big new resort hotels for white folks. This gave her money to feed her students who brought their own pallets and slept on the floor. She saved the wrappings on things bought at the store and used it for writing paper. She made ink from boiled elderberries growing near the house, and she made pens from feather quills of the neighbors' barnyard fowls. Her motto for her students was, "Enter to learn: Depart to serve." These words were, years later, to be cut into the stone portal of her school.

One of the winter vacationers from the north was John Gamble, a soap manufacturer who became a loyal supporter for Mary's school. Another was Thomas White, a maker of sewing machines. She often brought her pupils to sing outside the hotel gates to thank the visitors for their gifts to her school which became the Daytona Educational and Normal Training School.

Word of Mary's successes reached education leaders of the nation for she was now also conducting night courses for adults in reading, writing, mathematics, civics, and home making.

Later she was to establish and gain support for the first hospital for the black people of Daytona, naming it for her father. So, Sam McLeod, who had been born a nameless slave, gave the borrowed name of his owner to a hospital that was to serve the black people for twenty years until the city built a new one.

Mary McLeod Bethune was the founder of the National Council of Negro Women. She served as the director of the American Red Cross in the state of Florida. She was president of the Association for the study of Negro Life and History. Under President Roosevelt's administration she served as director of the Negro Affairs Division of the National Youth Administration, and as a consultant to the founding conference of the United Nations. After the president died, Mrs. Roosevelt presented his cane to Mrs. Bethune in recognition of her work. She used the cane until her death.

Regarding the struggling boys and girls of the generations to follow her, Mary McLeod said, "I can never rest while there is still something that I can do to make the ground firmer under their feet, to make their efforts more productive, to bring their goals nearer, to make their faith in God and their fellow men a little stronger."

Speaking directly to the youth of America, she reminded them, "The doors of progress and advancement will open to the steady, persistent pressure of your skilled hands and your trained minds, your stout hearts and your prayers, more readily than they opened to me. I rejoice (at age seventy-five) in the movement for the extended brotherhood through greater interracial understanding. I rejoice that I have been able to demonstrate that there is a place in God's sun for the Youth who has vision, the determination, and the courage to reach it."

Julia, Fanny and Catherine
Cooks, cookbooks, and kitchens

Have you ever switched on your television set and wished that what you were seeing was going on in your own kitchen? Someone was putting an egg pudding in the oven and calling it a "Quiche." It was so delicious looking that your taste buds began to water and you could almost smell it.

The name of that woman on the television screen was Julia Child, and she was so fascinating you watched every move as she demonstrated one of her cooking secrets. She has been known as T.V.'s French Chef.

Now Julia was not French, nor could she speak the language as a young woman. But when she moved to Paris with her husband she decided to learn about French cooking and enrolled in the famous Cordon Bleu Cooking School. The French were the first to combine art with cooking.

When she finished that six-month course, she started a cooking school for Americans in her own apartment, assisted by two French women. During this time, Julia realized there was a need for a guide with step-by-step instructions for cooking in the French manner, called French cuisine. It took her ten years to complete it, but when her book, Mastering the Art of French Cooking, was published in 1961, she became instantly popular as a French Chef.

One of her first television appearances on a Boston station was to demonstrate how to cook an omelet on a small hot plate. She was so charming and made it seem so easy, that within a few months she was doing weekly programs demonstrating tempting recipes in a full size kitchen on a T.V. stage. Viewers, enchanted with her friendly and easy style, hurried to their own kitchens to try the mouth watering ideas. Men and women, both, began making omelets in the Julia Child Way.

With over one hundred television channels carrying her program, thousands of families across America who were viewing her programs or reading her book, were eating much better and enjoying it more.

Julia's instructions for measuring ingredients in a recipe were usually precise. One-half teaspoon of this and one full teaspoon of that, or two tablespoons of these and one cup of those.

But it was not always so easy for one cook to follow another's directions so precisely. Sometimes things didn't come out right. A woman telling her sister how to make a certain cake would say, "Add a handful of sugar." A mother showing her son how to make fudge would say, "Add a pinch of salt." Now, the sister's tiny hand may hold less than her larger sister's hand, and the son's athletic fingers may "pinch" a larger amount than his mother's dainty fingers. So, in the early days of America, food was prepared and cooked in somewhat of a guessing game manner.

About 1900, a woman named Fannie Farmer decided to do something about this. She started a School of Cookery which was to become famous. Most of her students were society women who had paid cooks in their kitchens to prepare and serve the meals. But on the cook's day off the family had to be fed. So the society matron herself went into the kitchen and attempted to put a meal together. To teach these women, Fannie Farmer decided to make her lectures simple and to use exact measurements in writing a cookbook. To avoid tragedies in the kitchen with a guessing method, she suggested simple, easy recipes using precise level measurements for all ingredients. From then on results in the kitchen were more edible.

Fannie Farmer had made an easy science out of home cooking. Her book sold over four million copies, and her name was popular in many kitchens.

Many years before the days of Fannie and Julia, another woman with vision and foresight realized something needed to be done to assist the busy American homemaker. Back in the 1800's, taking care of a home and family required tremendous and numerous tasks. Wood had to be brought in for the kitchen stove and the fireplace to warm the house. Water had to be pumped and lifted in buckets on to the large kitchen stove to be heated for cooking and bathing. Baking was done in a small section of the wood-burning stove where the heat was uneven and temperatures for baking were unpredictable. Cooking of meats, over one hundred years ago, depended upon the size of the stove and the type of metal pots found in the kitchen.

Catherine Beecher knew all about these tasks and decided to make them more pleasant. In spite of that nineteenth century lack of modern plumbing, heating, and cooking, she created labor-saving devices and methods.

She believed there was a science to housekeeping and prepared a guide which illustrated her ideas. It included convenient floorplans for rooms, especially the kitchen. She designed a kitchen stove with a roasting oven at one end, a baking section enclosed on the top of the stove, and even some storage space.

With her sister Harriet Beecher Stow, a famous author, Catherine Beecher wrote the practical guide to housekeeping, called The American Woman's Home. This book demonstrated that running a house efficiently required training and gave dignity and great importance to the main occupation of the women of America in the 1800's.

Catherine II the Great
Wise Empress of Russia

Her name was changed from Sophia to Catherine at her betrothal as a little German princess to the heir of the Russian crown.

Young and shy, and thinking herself dull and ugly, poor little unloved Sophia was later to be known as Catherine II, the Grand Duchess and Empress of Russia.

Although she was a princess, her family never had much money. Her father, Prince Christian August of Anawalt-Zerbst, was a general in the service of King Frederick, but he received very little money for his service as governor of the dull and cold city of Strettin on the Baltic Sea.

Sophia's mother was Johanna, Princess of Holstein-Gottorp, who was distantly related to the Empress of Russia. Having grown up in one of the most elegant courts in Europe, Johanna wanted her children to have more than was offered in uninteresting and windy Strettin.

Sophia learned all the arts required of a young lady and much of the courtly behavior demanded of a princess. She had lessons in French, spelling, religion, history, and music. Some she enjoyed; others she hated. She frequently annoyed her teachers with argumentative questions.

From her austere yet kind father, Sophia learned compassion, justice, and the value of truth. In that eighteenth century the world was full of frivolity and inequality. But she learned from her father, the religious Prince, the basic principles of democracy.

In those days marriages of young children were arranged by parents and relatives. Particularly was it necessary that a young princess be promised to a young man of a wealthy and influential family, especially if she were poor and not too attractive. No matter her brilliant mind and culture, women were to be ladies, to be waited upon, to walk in the gardens and gossip, to dance and play games, but rarely to rule or to participate in decisions of government. However, the title of Catherine the Great was to become the future name of Sophia.

It was a cold day in February when the young girl named Sophia with her Princess mother arrived in Moscow having been promised by her father, a German prince, to be wed to her young cousin Peter.

Though a year older than Sophia, he was younger in character and he seemed very childish to her. However, she was extremely wise even as a young girl and made a friend of the young prince whom she must marry at all costs if she wished to become an empress.

At the same time Sophia realized that it was more the Empress, Peter's mother, whom she had to please since marriage of princes were decided by parents or other powerful persons. As required she devoted herself completely to the study of the Russian language and the Greek Orthodox religion. Being an intelligent and sensitive child she flung herself eagerly into the study and received high praise for her intelligence and zeal, thus pleasing the Empress.

Catherine made herself worthy of the title she coveted. Peter was weak, lazy, and terrified by the shadow of responsibility, and he did much to make himself unworthy to reign.

On the day of her betrothal the name Catherine was used for the first time. Sophia Augusta Fredericks received, in exchange for her three Christian names, the first name of Catherine to which was added the Russian patronymic Akexeivna. The wedding of Peter III to Catherine II was a national festival. More important than the questionable love of young Peter to Catherine was the imperial crown, which was placed upon her head. The elegant wedding dress is still on view in the Kremlin museum. The young couple, fragile and overawed, encrusted with silver and diamonds, were cheered with affection as they rode in gold carriages drawn by white horses.

When Catherine was thirty-three years old Peter's mother died. Peter and Catherine then inherited the throne of Russia in 1761 as Grand Duke and Duchess, Emperor and Empress of Russia.

By this time the unattractive and neglected little girl had become a tall and graceful woman. She had reached the peak of her beauty and mental powers. Her naturally wavy black hair, framed a face of dazzling white skin with large expressive blue eyes, long lashes, a Greek nose, and a smiling mouth.

Her joyous laugh, pleasant voice, and friendly manner

made her loved by everyone. Years of quiet observation and personal study had made her a brilliant woman who could explain complicated legal documents and who understood a network of intrigue between nations which was the way foreign policy worked in eighteenth century Europe.

Law and justice in Russia was primitive, cruel, and contradictory. No one was properly trained. Reform was needed. And Catherine did it.

Catherine's greatest desire was to provide equality of political and civil liberties for the serfs of slavery, who were the main force of labor in Russia, as well as for the nobility, who were often selfish, corrupt, and lazy.

She also won the respect and cooperation of rulers of other countries by her brilliant reign, her friendly manner, and her popular court pageantry where she allowed no gossip and no intrigue. Morale in her court was very high. Everyone loved the Empress.

Peter III, her husband, had become mentally and emotionally ill and had signed an abdication in 1762.

Catherine's reign provided the world with one of its most splendid and cultured capitals of the world at St. Petersburg, which today is known as Leningrad. Today visitors admire the building known as the Hermitage, then her winter palace. It contains one of the world's largest and most impressive art collections in the stunning setting of Catherine's gold court. That was the age of reason, and the idea of freedom was to spring from it. Catherine's principles of democracy became instruments which would abolish the nobility and monarchies and eventually provide freedom from serfdom for its masses. She gave to Russia its first taste of equality and justice.

Elinore, the Homesteader

American pioneer in the west

Her name was Elinore Pruitt Stewart. Most of her stories about homesteading in Wyoming appeared in letters to her friend and former employer, Juliet Coney of Denver.

She wrote of her days as a homesteader in the old west at the turn of the century. Combining range talk with a formal literary style of books she had read, she wrote of the daily work, of the wonders of nature, and of her love for her neighbors, though they were miles apart.

"I had never seen a pine until I came to Colorado. At that time I was hoping to pass the Civil Service examination, with no very definite idea as to what I would do, but just to be improving my time and opportunity. I never went to public school a day in my life. In my childhood there was no such thing in the Indian Territory of Oklahoma where we lived, so I had to try to keep learning. Before the time came for the examination I was so discouraged because of the grippe (an illness) that nothing but the mountains, the pines, and the clean, fresh air seemed worth while; so it all came about just as I have written. . .

"I am way up close to the Forest Reserve of Utah, within half a mile of the line, sixty miles from the railroad. I was twenty-four hours on the train and two days on the stage, and oh, those two days! The snow was just beginning to melt and the mud was the worst I ever heard of. The first stage we tackled was just about as rickety as it could very well be."

The trip to the land office to file claim took a whole week to go and come. She continued, "We camped out for there was but one house in the whole sixty miles, and not a tree to be seen, nothing but sage, sand and sheep . . . when we stopped to camp we raised the wagon tongue and spread the wagon sheet over it and made a bedroom on the warm, soft sand . . . As the moon came up I saw a coyote come trotting along and felt sorry for him, having to hunt food in so barren a place, but when I heard the whirr of wings I felt sorry for the sage chickens he had disturbed. . .

"After the haying season I decided on a day off so saddled the pony and left at sunup. A creek along the hills had groves of quaking asp and cottonwoods that made shade. We caught a few grasshoppers and I cut a birch pole for a rod. The trout were beautiful, their sides so silvery and speckles so black. They bite so well that it doesn't require any special skill or tackle to catch plenty in a few minutes. I made a fire first and then dressed the trout while it was burning down, and with native berries and some bread we had a feast."

On another occasion she describes the adventure of hunting jack rabbits and squirrels for food while on a camping trip in the mountains, and her dramatic report on the snow-slide made you feel you were there. Her goal of securing the final deed on her property was always before her. "It will be two years before I can get the deed. The five years in which I am required to prove up will have passed by then. Also, I am entitled to one hundred and sixty acres more. I shall file on that much some day when I have sufficient money of my own earning. The law requires a cash payment of twenty-five cents per acre at filing, and one dollar more per acre when final proof is made. I want to earn every cent that goes into my own land and improvements myself. I know I shall succeed; other women have. I know of several who are now where they can laugh at past trials. Do you know?—I am a firm believer in laughter. . ."

Our Homesteader concludes, "I never like to theorize, and so this year I set out to prove that a woman could ranch if she wanted to. We like to grow potatoes on new ground, that is, newly claimed land on which no crop has been grown. Few weeds grow on new land. I planted a garden and had almost an acre in vegetables. I irrigated and cultivated it myself. We had all the vegetables we could use and now have a cellar full.

"I milked ten cows a day all summer; I have sold enough butter to pay for a year's supply of flour and gasoline. We use a gasoline lamp. I have raised enough chickens to completely renew my flock, and all we wanted to eat and have some fryers for the winter, and turkeys for all the birthdays and holidays. I raised a great many flowers and I worked several days in the field. . . Of course, I am extra strong, but those who try know that strength and knowledge come from doing. I just love to experiment, to work, to prove out things, so that ranch life and 'roughing it' just suit me."

Marguerite Higgins, War Correspondent
More front page stories than any other reporter

The war correspondent whose face was more often covered with mud than with makeup was known as "Maggie." In World War II she carried major responsibilities while a mere beginner in the field of journalism. In the Korean War, she was the only woman on the front lines.

Marguerite Higgins accompanied the Seventh Army into Austria in 1945. She became so involved in everything that was going on that, as a result, she had more front page stories than any other reporter during the last six months of the war.

When war broke out in Korea, she was one of the first to get in. She said in June of 1950, "For me, to get to Korea was more than a story, it was a crusade, my newspaper's coverage of the war."

Sometime later, it was a much sadder Maggie who said upon the retreat of Seoul, "I walked out of Seoul, and I want to walk back in."

When General MacArthur sent her out of Korea, along with all the other women including nurses, she objected, "I am not working in Korea as a woman, I am here as a war correspondent."

However, she was put aboard the General's plane and again made most of the moment by interviewing him .

Maggie's good humor, agility, and bravery were the subject of frequent comment as she shared hardships on equal terms with soldiers and male correspondents. She was accredited with saving many lives of the seriously wounded by learning to administer blood plasma.

The small, slight blonde has been described as "winsome, alarmingly brave, extraordinarily durable, and pretty, even in fighting clothes." At the front she wore shirt, trousers, fatigue cap and tennis shoes. And she always carried a toothbrush, towel and lipstick.

During student days at the University of California from which she graduated with honors in 1941, Maggie secured a job as a cub reporter on the Vallejo Times Herald. While earning a Master's Degree in journalism at Columbia University in New York, she was campus correspondent for the New York Herald Tribune. In 1944, they sent her to their London Bureau. Maggie's fluency in French brought a transfer to Paris. She learned French when her father had married a French woman who arranged for her daughter's early education to be in French as well as in English.

From Paris she went to Austria, and later to Berlin, where in 1945, at the age of twenty-four, she became chief of the

Berlin bureau. A few years later came the Korean War and its accompanying correspondent responsibility.

Maggie's good humor, agility, and bravery were the subject the years following her experiences as war correspondent. Among them was the 1951 Pulitzer Prize in Journalism. These prizes were established under terms of the will of Joseph Pulitzer, American newspaper publisher. The prizes are awarded annually by the Trustees of Columbia University.

The only woman to serve on the Korean front lines wrote of her experiences in a book entitled, *War in Korea: the report of a Woman Combat Correspondent.*

Deborah and Lydia
Judge and Businesswoman of the Bible

With her hair blowing in the wind and her dark eyes flashing, she ordered the army down the side of Mt. Tabor to battle in the valley below. Although the enemy was much better equipped, her army was bigger.

In this battle which took place long before Christopher Columbus discovered America and even before Jesus Christ was born, the enemy had 900 chariots of iron drawn by swift horses, and she had an army of 10,000 foot soldiers with only the swords in their hands.

Who was this lovely general, so brave and so sure of her success in battle? She was a prophetess, and a leader and counselor of the people of Israel.

Deborah lived in the hill country of Ephraim near Bethel. As a prophetess, the people believed she had a message from God for them, and they went up to her for judgment. Assisting her in governing the land was Barak, a loyal leader whom the people liked.

When word came that a nearby king, named Jabin, was planning to attack her people and had assembled his chariot army under the leadership of a fierce general named Sisera, Deborah commanded Barak to gather together an army. He agreed to this providing she would go with him because he sensed that as a phophetess and inspired by God, she would bring victory in time of battle.

Her reply was, "I will surely go with you."

This battle was between the Israelites whom Deborah ruled and the Canaanites of King Jabin on the great plain of Esdraelon. It was an important location because it was a trade route where caravans passed bringing silks and candied fruit from Damascus to the south, pickled fish from the Sea of Galilee, and gold from Arabia to the north.

Barak gathered men from the tribes of Zebulun and Naphtali who lived near the Sea of Galilee. At the scene of battle hundreds from other tribes of Israel joined them also. In spite of those chariots of iron of King Jabin, Deborah urged her army forward by saying, "UP! For this is the day in which our God has delivered Sisera into your hands. Is not God gone out before you?"

A mysterious strength of will and muscle flowed through the ranks of the Israelites. They rushed forward, and it became a furious battle. Help suddenly came also from the sky in a blinding torrent of rain. The chariots of Sisera were bogged down in the mud. They became tangled and trapped, and

Barak's fighting men hit them from all sides in a hand-to-hand battle.

When the battle was over and won, and the people were called together to give thanks to God, Deborah sang a song of victory:

"They fought from heaven;
The stars in their courses fought against Sisera."

This historic battle is told in the Bible in the Book of Judges in Chapters four and five, in two versions, one in prose, the other in poetry. Chapter five is often called the Song of Deborah. It is one of the most precious and one of the oldest literary legacies of ancient times, believed to have been written about 1150 B.C., and inserted later in the Book of Judges in the Old Testament of the Bible.

After that decisive battle in which a woman led her army on to victory, there were forty years of peace for the people of Israel.

LYDIA

A thousand years after that fierce battle the whole country, and, indeed, all the land bordering the eastern end of the Mediterranean Sea, experienced considerable change in life style and culture.

Far to the north, near Philippi, in northern Greece, a businesswoman had developed a fine reputation and many customers. She was known as Lydia, a "seller of purple."

Lydia probably sold cloth which had been dyed purple, a favorite color although the shade of color varied from our modern idea of royal purple to shades of blue-green. The term royal purple is very appropriate. Because of the high cost of processing purple dye, only the very rich or royal persons could afford purple cloth.

Purple dye was obtained from a substance in the neck-gland of shellfish. The dyeing of cloth was an intricate process and required several people, some equipment, and some money to get started and to keep the business going. Because of her occupation Lydia held an important position in the community.

Philippi was a large commercial center, a crossroads of traders from the East and the West, near the seacoast town of Neopolis. Today that seacoast city is known as Kavala, and the archaeological ruins of the great old city of Philippi are a few miles inland. There were excellent transportation connections in the center of the dyeing industry, and Lydia was conducting her business as a prominent member of Philippian society. But Lydia closed down her business on the Sabbath, as did the loyal Jews.

It was on one of these days when she was resting alongside a lovely singing stream with members of her large household that Lydia met Paul. He was on a missionary journey to Philippi seeking all who would listen to his remarkable story of the birth of Christianity and the new Christian Church.

Paul had been looking for a synagog in Philippi but found none. Hebrew law specified that ten Jewish men must be present to open a place of worship. There may not have been that many in Philippi. Or, it may have been that when the Jews were expelled from Rome, the city of Philippi, which also was under Roman law, followed the same decree requiring the Jews to worship outside the city walls.

So Paul and his friends, Luke, Silas, and Timothy, walked into the countryside to find a place of prayer. They sat down along the little creek and talked to the women who had gathered there. Perhaps they commented on the beautiful wild flowers which grew along the creek bank—tiny pinks and bright blue corn flowers.

While the men talked, Lydia listened. Their message impressed her. Later she became converted to their faith and was baptized. Then she arranged to have her whole household baptized also.

Lydia opened her home to Paul and his friends. Even after Paul was jailed in Philippi and released he returned to visit in her home.

Lydia and her household may have been the nucleus of that first church in Philippi. It flourished and became one of the greatest centers of Christianity in the Mediterranean area.

This account of Lydia, the businesswoman, "Seller of Purple," and friend of Christianity, is found in the book of Acts, Chapter 16, of the New Testament of the Bible.

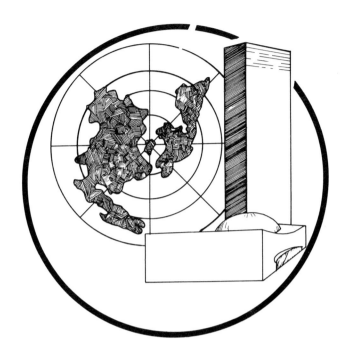

United Nations Leaders
At the top of the world's organization

Women have made it to the United Nations! To the presidencies of two of the world's most important organizations, the General Assembly and the Security Council of the United Nations.

A lady lawyer from Liberia in Africa, whose name was Angie E. Brooks, enlivened assembly procedings when she became President of the 24th session of the General Assembly in 1969. As a past president of the International Federation of Women's Lawyers she has been a sturdy battler for the rights of African peoples, with special emphasis on women.

In 1954 Mrs. Vyaya Lakshmi Pandit, sister of Jawaharlal Nehru of India, was the only other woman to serve in that post.

In 1972 the first woman of the UN Security Council was elected. Jeanne Martin Cisse of Guinet in Africa, is a mother of six children. She believed women better qualified when they were mothers because they naturally loved peace and security.

In addition to these international leaders dozens of other women serve their countries in the United Nations. International Women's Year was proclaimed in 1975.

With the proclamation of the Universal Declaration of Human Rights, which says that "everyone is entitled to all the rights and freedoms set forth in this Declaration, without distinction of any kind, such as race, color, sex, language, religion, political or other opinion, national or socal origin, property, birth, or other status" the principle of equality for men and women has come to be accepted by the community of nations. It has been written into the constitutions and legislation of many member states. Many laws, regulations and practices which once discriminated against women have been repealed or amended. In the great majority of countries women vote and are elected to office as part of the regular process of government. There are women in parliaments and congresses and even some judges. Several serve as ambassadors, mayors of large cities, on school boards, as commissioners and other local government authorities, as civil servants and as jurors.

In most countries schools are open to girls. The number of professional women shows their acceptance is rarely prohibited by law but rather by deeply rooted attitudes. Several countries have investigated conditions of employment of women, have enacted equal pay and other legislation and have taken action to remove economic discrimination based on sex.

There have been new laws in status of women regarding married women, consent of marriage, age of marriage, property rights and guardianship of children. This proves some distance covered, but much more remains to be achieved. Several member states of the United Nation have been adjusting their laws and customs, and the scope and content varies from country to country. The studies prepared for the Commission on the Status of Women of the United Nations, the debates at the Commission's annual sessions and the seminars held under the advisory services program are means through which methods and experiences are exchanged.

The Commission which came into existance in June 1946 has brought about the recognition of many distinguished women. Representing their governments have been women judges, diplomats, professors, senior civil servants and members of parliament, working together in activities at national and international levels.

The Commission meets once each year for a session of three weeks. The meeting place is either in New York or in Geneva, Switzerland.

Thus, the United Nations acts at the international level to encourage and supplement the efforts of governments and organizations, but the goal will be reached with the faith, encouragement and cooperation of men and women everywhere.

Some National Characteristics

The women leaders who were selected from their own countries to the United Nations were, in a way, representative of women from all over the world. They were individuals who had won respect and confidence to be leaders of others.

In a similar manner, other women such as those we have read about in this book were outstanding individuals of achievement. Many of them brought a lasting influence to their work and contribution to the world. They had moral courage, and ideals and principles which have enriched people everywhere.

There are also certain women who represent an interesting style of culture from their own land or country. They display national characteristics. Some of these have been included in the next chapters.

The Fashion World of Africa

Let's peak at the fashion world of women of Africa. There are styles and tastes of greater variety than anywhere else in the world.

Although numerous city dwellers have gone European in their dress, many women still wear traditional native costume. Let's look in on the wardrobe of three women of three completely different countries on that large African continent.

In Ethiopia she wears purest white. In Nigeria, it's deepest blue. In South Africa, it's beads and wire.

The attractive lovely golden-skinned woman from East Africa wears the shamma, a gauzimer white wraparound with a colorfully embroidered border. This is the national costume for both sexes and all ages. The garment is a rectangular shawl exceeding three yards in length, handwoven and made of cotton. The women drape the white shamma over shirt-like dresses with very full skirts to the ankle. These dresses are often made of beautifully colored materials, in addition to the white color of the shamma shawl.

If the garment has a wide red stripe near the hem, it is called jano and is worn on feast days. It is also folded differently.

The women may wrap a cloak, called a barnos, over their shoulders especially in the cool evenings. They are often richly ornamented and lined with leather.

Most of the Ethiopians go barefooted, but some wear sandals. Some cover their heads with a hood attached to the barnos. Small umbrellas, woven from grass or reeds, are sometimes carried as protection against rain or sun.

For jewelry, the white clad woman from Ethiopia might display an elaborately hand wrought Coptic Cross in Silver or a pendant of an elephant's tooth, and a bracelet of lion's claws.

The lady from the western African coast is probably a member of the Yoruba tribe of Nigeria. It is one of the largest and most advanced of the African groups. They were living in large well-organized communities long before the arrival of the Europeans. These women are generally distinguished by their blue dresses and turbans. The very full skirts are made of handwoven fabric colored with traditional indigo dyes. A turban, also of blue, is attractively arranged to cover most of the head.

The Bantu women of South Africa wear long aprons or skirts, hanging down in front and back from the waist. Among the many Bantu tribes, the Nguni women wear a bodice across the breasts and under the armpits, but in other groups the upper part of the body is left uncovered. In cold weather cloaks of soft skin or fur, carefully made and decorated, are added to the ordinary dress. Only members of the royal family may wear leopard or lions skins.

Young girls wear short fringes of skins, beadwork, or vegetable fibre. Older girls wear fringes or aprons reaching to the knees. Among the Sotho tribe the apron is longer in back. Among the Venda tribe the women wear a lionskin brought between the legs and tucked behind into the waist girdle to hang down in a flap.

Flat sandals of oxhide are worn attached to the foot by a thong, and caps of skin or fur are worn in the winter season.

Babies are carried on the back in cradleskins slung around the waist and knotted over the breast. Babies are often naked except for a bead or string girdle and occasional necklace or charm.

Ornaments used by Bantu women are mainly beads and wire of iron or copper of varying thicknesses twisted into bracelets worn around the neck, arms, and ankles. Certain kinds of copper bracelets and ornaments are worn only by women of rank among the Venda and Sotho tribes. Beads are worked into headbands, necklaces, breast ornaments, waistbands, and bracelets. Ivory bracelets are prerogative of rank in most tribes.

The Zulus have developed a language of the beads with different combinations of colors and patterns having conventional meanings attached to them. For example, if a young woman receives a certain arrangement of colored beads in a necklace, it may convey a message of love, and that means she must respond with an answer.

The Bedouin Maiden

Not far from the African continent live the women of the Bedouin tribes in the countries known as the Middle East. They live in Syria, Lebanon, and Israel at the eastern end of the Mediterranean Sea.

The Bedouin Maiden stood in the narrow entrance of her family's black tent on the warm sand of the Syrian desert. The bristley hairs of the woven goat-hair cloth pricked her arm, and she straightened in the early morning light. Her gaze was toward the east where her father had just rounded the dry barren hills, his flock maneuvering behind him.

She stood quietly as the morning sunshine carressed her face and neck and her long arms where the plain dark dress with its ragged edges exposed her beautiful olive skin. These early hours were her favorite time before the heat of the day in the treeless land drove everyone inside, under the long low squatty dark tents which Bedouins call home.

It wouldn't be long, she mused, before her mother called her to take the earthen vessel down to the small well for the day's supply of water. If she delayed long enough she might find there a certain shepherd boy leading his flock over the rocky hillside. He had been there on previous mornings. Perhaps she would be lucky this morning. He came a long distance from his Bedouin tent because none were within view of her family's area. So she set out this particular morning adjusting the earthen vessel more comfortably on her head. As she walked the long path to the well her mind was on the lovely custom of the desert people when a daughter of one tent family is given in marriage to a son of another tent family.

Tradition is strong among these Bedouin people near the Dead Sea. They still live in the manner of their forefathers, even back to Abraham, one of the great men written about in the Old Testament. The importance of marriage, family and female chastity is greatly magnified. A Bedouin maiden who transgresses is put to death.

But the festival of a wedding supercedes all other activity. A procession is led by a single camel carrying the bride and her mother on the way to the home of the husband-to-be. The mother holds a flag aloft, even if only an old bandana on a stick. The music is, of course, from the versatile bamboo shepherd's pipe. Whatever horses and donkeys can be added become part of the procession along with adults and children walking, singing, and capering as they go, often expelling the shrill wedding cries.

At sunset the wedding feast is prepared, merely enough to

eat, for these Bedouin can rarely afford to slaughter their herd.
A wedding dance line continues into the night around the tent
where the bride in her finery is secluded. In serpentine fashion
the men and boys sing as they go, occasionally stopping to face
one another in rhythmic stampings and clappings.

The bride is usually dressed in the finest clothing she may
ever again wear in her life. Dark silk, embroidered with gilt,
is covered with a long dark veil, and her face is partially covered. She may be wearing some form of jewelry, perhaps a
series of brightly colored bracelets. However, within the week
she will probably be dressed once again in the plain ragged
clothing of the female members of the family. As a new daugh-
ter-in-law custom places her in the family not much higher
than a donkey.

The price a man pays for a bride may require many sales
of wool from his sheep, but in the Bedouin custom of family
importance, one hundred fifty or two hundred dollars is worth
the joy of a healthy wife who is capable of working hard and
bearing many children.

The Japanese Bride

Traveling further east from the African women of fashion and the Bedouin maidens we come to a country known for its beautiful cherry blossoms and its famous snow-capped Mount Fuji.

In Japan the women still wear colorful kimonos and obis (large sashes) although many have changed to western dress as it is worn in America and Europe.

One of the greatest events in the life of a young Japanese woman is the day she becomes a bride and the celebration which follows.

For centuries it was customary for parents to arrange marriages for their sons and daughters. It is still done in some

families today. Less frequently, however, in the latter half of
the twentieth century, are marriages arranged by go-betweens,
usually a trusted friend of the family. The westernized youth
of post World War II in Japan are more independent and
experience a social freedom not known to the former generations.

In the arranged marriages, a friend is asked to plan for
the boy and girl to meet. It is usually at a party or picnic. If
they are interested in one another, they exchange gifts. If one
keeps the other's gifts, it has meaning—they are engaged to be
married.

The wedding in Japan has high priority among family
affairs and frequently lasts for several days. No religious sanc-
tion is required. Formerly the ceremony was conducted in the
home of the bridegroom. Recently, however, weddings have
been held in Shinto shrines, the center of the ancient and still-
venerated worship of nature and ancestors. The shrine ceremony includes white-robed priests and black-hatted musicians
who play archaic music composed centuries ago for the imperial
court. The most solemn moment of the Shinto wedding occurs
when the groom promises the gods to assume the responsibility
of marriage. The bride kneels demurely beside her husband
before an altar laden with offerings. She is dressed in a costly
silk robe; over her heavy wig a white silk tsunokakushi (horn
concealer) symbolizes her promise to avoid jealousy.

The high point of the ceremony is called the sansankudo,
literally "three, three, nine times." The custom requires that
the bride and groom take three sips of cold sake, pronounced
"sahkee," from each of three lacquered cups. A smiling atten-
dant pours sake into the first cup. The bride drinks the sake in
three sips, the cup is refilled and passed to the bridegroom, who
does the same. When the second cup is offered, it is the groom

who sips before the bride. But the bride again drinks first from the third cup. Since three is considered a lucky number and nine the luckiest, the combination helps explain why, with this rite, the marriage is finally solemnized.

Following the sansankudo, a banquet and entertainment are provided with the bride and groom seated with the go-between and his wife, if it was an arranged marriage. For the banquet the bride changes her bridal robe for a vivid kimono and dons a different wig that indicates matronly status. The lavish meal includes a clam soup, hamaguri, whose coupled shells symbolize the union. To make it clear to the assembled group who the principal characters are, lettered napkins in the front of the red lacquered trays serving the couple mean bride and groom.

Elaborate picture taking follows, usually in some exquisite garden. Rows of small boxes, each daintily wrapped and all identical are stacked neatly and left unopened during the festivities. Some hours later, when the joyous but weary guests start home, tucked under each arm is one of the daintily wrapped boxes, a reminder of the wedding day, a gift from the bride and groom.